THE LITTLE BOOK OF
NEWCASTLE UNITED

Independent and Unofficial

FOURTH EDITION

EDITED BY
DAVID CLAYTON

MIX
Paper | Supporting
responsible forestry
FSC® C020056

First published by Carlton Books in 2003

This updated edition published in 2023 by OH! An Imprint of Welbeck
Non-Fiction Limited, part of Welbeck Publishing Group.
Offices in: London – 20 Mortimer Street, London W1T 3JW
and Sydney – Level 17, 207 Kent St, Sydney NSW 2000 Australia
www.welbeckpublishing.com

Compilation text © Welbeck Non-Fiction Limited 2023
Design © Welbeck Non-Fiction Limited 2023

ISBN 978 1 80069 553 5

Updated edition compiled by: David Clayton
Project manager: Russell Porter
Production: Jess Brisley

A CIP catalogue record of this book is available from the British Library.

Printed in China

10 9 8 7 6 5 4 3 2 1

CONTENTS

INTRODUCTION

There is no other club like Newcastle Untied. For over 130 years the Magpies have found new ways to amaze, frustrate, delight and exasperate their life-long supporters.

This book attempts the impossible task of conveying that history via a collection of quotes, both from the greats and from those best forgotten. But in the end there's only really one, universally acknowledged, quote about this club that needs to be recorded:

"Howay the lads!"

CHAPTER 1

THE NEWCASTLE WAY

Passion for the shirt, passion for the city...

"It was agreed that the club's colours should be changed from red shirts and white knickers to black-and-white shirts (two-inch stripe) and dark knickers. **"**

Minutes of club meeting, 2 August 1894

NEWCASTLE UNITED

“ This is a fantastic football club with great spirit and a public that live, breathe and die for everything that goes on here. **”**

A defiant **BOBBY ROBSON**
after United's loss to Partizan Belgrade, 2003

"They talk about Newcastle being a sleeping giant but it was more comatose than asleep.**"**

Local journalist **BOB CASS**, *1992*

"Vaya cuidad – what a town!**"**

TINO ASPRILLA *after his first visit to*
Newcastle's famous Bigg Market

❝ If we invite any player up to the quayside to see the girls and then up to our magnificent stadium, we will be able to persuade any player to sign. **❞**

BOBBY ROBSON

on the myriad attractions of Tyneside

" Newcastle is a nice city to live in.
I was surprised because I had heard many
legends about England. About the weather,
the food and the time everything closes.
But I loved it. **"**

BOBBY CHARLTON

❝At Newcastle I was older than the manager, older than the assistant manager, older than the physio and the club doctor – which must be some sort of record. **❞**

STUART PEARCE

recounts life as captain of Newcastle's Dad's Army

"We're like the Basques.
We are fighting for a nation, the
Geordie nation. Football is tribalism
and we're the Mohicans. **"**

SIR JOHN HALL, *1995*

‟ You know what Newcastle are like. You never know what's going to happen. **”**

KENNY DALGLISH *after a Shearer-inspired*
4–3 win over Leicester City

❝ Our prices are half Newcastle's prices – you just can't compare the clubs, they're not to compare. We're stuck between a massive city that's vibrant like Newcastle… and Middlesbrough. **❞**

Sunderland chairman **BOBBY MURRAY**
and his envy of Tyneside, 2002

"To call football religion is too much.
But there's no doubt that, in places like
Newcastle, when they've got a good
team and are playing well, then the spirits
of the people are lifted. **"**

CARDINAL BASIL HUME

on football's place in the scheme of things

"Of all 22 I was the only player born within the city walls and north of the Tyne. These lads from Durham and Chester-Le-Street don't count.**"**

Boyhood Toon fan **DENIS TUEART** *after scoring the winner for Manchester City in the 1976 League Cup final*

NEWCASTLE UNITED

" Good evening, Newcastle! **"**

DAVID BOWIE
greets the crowd from the stage of...
Roker Park, Glass Spider Tour, 23 June 1987

❝So Brighton kick off this historic match and, as you sample the quite unique atmosphere here at St James' Park, you wonder how British football let alone Newcastle United will ever replace Kevin Keegan. **❞**

Commentator **ALAN PARRY**, *1984*

"Nobody hands you cups on a plate.**"**

TERRY MCDERMOTT,

number two to Kevin Keegan

"The people here love their football and, if you play for Newcastle, they see you as a very special person.**"**

NOLBERTO SOLANO

ff Of all the clubs I played for, I still get tingles down the back of my neck thinking about Newcastle. **jj**

MICKEY QUINN,
former NUFC striker

"The pinnacle of my career has to be wearing the number nine for Newcastle, probably the most famous shirt in British football. I still have one stored under my bed.**"**

TONY CUNNINGHAM,
crowd favourite of the 1980s

❝ Like selling the family silver… **❞**

Chairman **GORDON MCKEAG**

on giving up control of the club

"My eventual dream is to have 11 Geordies playing for Newcastle United and 11 in the reserves.**"**

SIR JOHN HALL

"The only Irishman who didn't know where Dublin was."

Unnamed reporter on Radio 5 Live after Shay Given failed to spot Coventry's No.9 lurking when he put the ball down in his own area. Dublin scored…

" Mr Keegan, I've never seen such quality football played at such a pace in my life. **"**

Royal Antwerp coach, **URBAIN HAESAERT***,*
after NUFC's 5–0 win in Belgium, 13 September 1994

❝With all those replica strips in the stands, coming to Newcastle is like playing in front of 40,000 baying zebras. **❞**

Tottenham manager **OSSIE ARDILES**
on failing to get Philippe Albert, signed by Kevin Keegan

"The best stadium in England and the best atmosphere in the Premier League. When we play at our home, it's like playing with 12, always. The support is fantastic. It's very hard to play against us here, with our fans so close to the pitch.**"**

BRUNO GUIMARÃES *– happy to be a Magpie!*
October 2022

"We're very happy to have won the Cup. Every man in Newcastle has done his duty.**"**

Captain **JIMMY NELSON**,
collecting the FA Cup after the 1932 final

❝We were a team in the best sense of the word. There were no superstars. No world-beaters, just a damned good team.**❞**

JIMMY SCOTT, *who played all 12 games in the Fairs Cup-winning run of 1968–69, and scored the club's first-ever goal in European competition*

CHAPTER 2

LEGENDS

**If you
make it on
Tyneside,
you're a
legend for
life...**

"I have been sold like a slave for a bag of gold.**"**

HUGHIE GALLACHER

reacts badly to being transferred to Chelsea, 1930

" Hughie of the Magic Feet is Dead. **"**

*Headline in the **NEWCASTLE JOURNAL***
following the suicide of Hughie Gallacher, 12 June 1957,

"And they were lucky to get none."

LEN SHACKLETON

after the 13–0 defeat of Newport County, 5 October 1946

Heroes are perfect – Jackie (Milburn) was perfect.

KEVIN KEEGAN

on the abrupt curtailment of his England career

" Jackie Milburn was a fine player –
he was quick, he was fast, he had a
change of pace, he could play
outside-right or centre-forward. **"**

STANLEY MATTHEWS

paying tribute to a former England colleague

❝I was worried to death that no one would turn up. Ten years is a long time. People forget.**❞**

JACKIE MILBURN

on his 1967 testimonial. Nearly 46,000 attended! Newcastle fans have long memories

❝ This is the only club I'd come back
to just to sweep the terraces. **❞**

JIM ILEY,

Magpies stalwart of the 1960s

❝I felt that I understood then what Tyneside was all about – it needed somebody to stick the ball in the net.**❞**

MALCOLM MACDONALD

reflecting on his home debut hat-trick against Liverpool,
21 August 1971

❝I remember crouching down and crying at the end of the game and Bill Shankly came across and he put his arm around me and said, 'Dinnae worry, son, you'll get there one day'.**❞**

MALCOLM MACDONALD

remembers the 1974 FA Cup final

"Surely Bobby Robson could have phoned me. After being involved in the international set-up for ten years, surely I'm worth a ten-pence phone call.**"**

KEVIN KEEGAN

on the abrupt curtailment of his England career

"The chant from the crowd, if you can follow the Geordie accents, appears to be, 'Bobby Robson, are you watching on the box?'**"**

Commentator **TONY GUBBA**
as Keegan scored four at Rotherham after being dropped by England manager Robson

❝If Newcastle win promotion, forget about making Kevin Keegan Player of the Year – he'll deserve to be named Team of the Year. They should rename Newcastle, Keegan United.**❞**

BOB PAISLEY, *Liverpool boss, November 1983*

"Whatever I've given Tyneside,
it's given me a hundred times as much.
I hope I'm always their friend and
I can tell them one thing – they'll always
be my friends up here.**"**

KEVIN KEEGAN'S

retirement speech after his final game for Newcastle, 1984

❝When I was a young boy I wanted to play for Newcastle United, I wanted to wear the number nine shirt and I wanted to score goals at St James' Park. I've lived my dream and I realise how lucky I've been to have done that. **❞**

ALAN SHEARER

reflects on finishing his career with the club he loves, 2006

❝I was very happy, not angry, when
I scored and I always celebrate in an unusual
way. I threw it to a good fan and I would
have got another from the bench. I knew
what I was doing. Everyone congratulated
me in the dressing room.**❞**

TEMURI KETSBAIA

on his manic hoarding-abusing goal celebration versus Bolton, 1998

" As soon as I walked into the ground I was greeted by the statue of former striker Malcolm Macdonald. "

DAVID GINOLA

gets his numéro neufs confused – he of course meant Jackie Milburn

❝It will always rankle with me that we didn't take the title after being so close, but I maintain that Manchester United won it rather than us losing it.**❞**

ROB LEE

on the lasting disappointment of season 1995–96, when the wrong United won the title

"The Newcastle Chairman Sir John Hall
went on the record to claim that
Les Ferdinand would be leaving
Newcastle 'over my dead body' –
I wonder if he is still alive.**"**

LES FERDINAND

❝I'm just a sheet metal worker's son from Gosforth. **❞**

ALAN SHEARER, *local hero, 1996*

"I wanted to wear that number nine shirt and nothing was going to derail me from getting it.**"**

ALAN SHEARER

❝ The two seasons we played together at Newcastle were like Heaven. **❞**

'SIR' LES FERDINAND

on his devastating partnership with Alan Shearer

"When he first came he wanted to get a fishing boat, so they took him to Tynemouth the first weekend he was here. He took one look at the North Sea and said, 'F**k that!'**"**

TINO ASPRILLA'S *interpreter* **NICK EMERSON**

"I'll be bringing the pigeons up to Newcastle with me, but I'll have to bring them up in the car. They're not good enough to find their own way here yet!**"**

Bird-fancier **DUNCAN FERGUSON**
at his first Newcastle press conference

"I may have looked calm, but my backside was going some."

ALAN SHEARER

after his successful penalty in the FA Cup semi-final v Spurs,
11 March 1999

“Next morning I decided to have it out with the manager. Dunc (Duncan Ferguson) had beaten me to it and the door to the manager's office was already off its hinges when I got to the training ground.**”**

ALAN SHEARER

remembering a rare occasion when Duncan Ferguson used his pace to good effect

" There was no hiding the fact that me and Ruud didn't see eye to eye, but I was as surprised as anyone when I heard the news. I always said no individual is bigger than any football club. "

ALAN SHEARER'S *reaction to Gullit's departure three days after losing the Tyne-Wear derby*

" He saved my career in a way, because I was down in the dumps when he came to Newcastle – he got me back to playing the way that I know I can. **"**

ALAN SHEARER *on Bobby Robson*

"Happy Birthday – any chance of a rise?"

Message from **ALAN SHEARER**
in a card marking Sir Bobby Robson's 70th birthday

❝The manager said at half time if I got six he might give me a Mars bar. I'll have to go out and buy my own now, won't I? **❞**

ALAN SHEARER

on "only scoring five" against Sheffield Wednesday
in an 8–0 success

"I wanted to score goals at St James' Park. I've lived my dream and I realise how lucky I've been to have done that.**"**

Injury forces **ALAN SHEARER**
to retire early, April 2006

"Alan Shearer has been the best striker in the Premiership.**"**

ALAN HANSEN,

the former Match of the Day *legend, shares a popular opinion*

"I'm a very happy man tonight.
I know what Jackie means and meant to the
people. I can now sleep easy that the
pressure has gone. **"**

ALAN SHEARER

*grabs his 201st United goal in February 2006, breaking Jackie
Milburn's Newcastle goalscoring record*

❝It's been everything I hoped for and more playing for Newcastle. The only – and it's a big only – thing that's missing is the silverware. Everything else has been fantastic.**❞**

ALAN SHEARER

"I first saw Gazza when he was 14.
He was talented, but so slow we wondered
if he could get round the pitch. But he grew,
lost the puppy fat and became quicker.
Very strong, with the vision, flair and
character to go with it. **"**

CHRIS WADDLE

on the ultimate entertainer, Gazza

❝I witnessed Gazza from a young age and what an incredible player. His enthusiasm was so infectious and the whole squad took so much from him during Italia 90. **❞**

PETER BEARDSLEY

– not a bad player himself for the Magpies and England

❝The ideal footballer, technically and socially. Great value; never a dull moment. **❞**

CHRIS WADDLE
on Gazza

❝Quite simply the best midfielder I've ever played with. In fact, he had the ability to be the best player in the world. **❞**

'SIR' LES FERDINAND

waxes lyrical about the genius of Gazza

❝No one can be the next Gazza.**❞**

PAUL GASCOIGNE

on, erm, Paul Gascoigne!

CHAPTER 3

GAFFERS TAKES: PART 1

**Managers, investors
or owners – being
in charge at
St James' Park
has never
been dull!
And a sense
of humour is
mandatory...**

❝He's just handed in a written transfer request. The handwriting was beautiful. **❞**

KENNY DALGLISH

on David Ginola

"I know the players I want.
It is like I have them in the fridge waiting
to come out. **"**

RUUD GULLIT

gives his current squad the cold shoulder

" We're developing our youth policy. **"**

KENNY DALGLISH

after Ian Rush joined fellow veteran John Barnes in Toon

"If you asked what would be my one wish, it would be to go back to England and, in one mad, great year, take over one club and win the championship. And I'd feel, well, I'd done it. **"**

Then manager of Porto, **BOBBY ROBSON**
hints at a return to the old country

❝A great appointment. He obviously loves the club, which is really important. I'm not saying Kenny Dalglish and Ruud Gullit didn't love the club, but Bobby knows the place, because it's in his heart – and I think that is a massive advantage.**❞**

KEVIN KEEGAN

on Bobby Robson's appointment

❝ It's lovely that he's in charge of his hometown club and that pride just oozes out of him. **❞**

BRIAN CLOUGH

gets sentimental about Bobby Robson

“ We mustn't be despondent.
We don't have to play them every
week – although we do play them
next week as it happens. **”**

BOBBY ROBSON *after a 2–0 league defeat to*
Arsenal who United faced a week later in the FA Cup

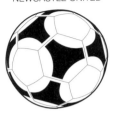

" We've got to batten down the hatches, plug a few leaks and get the ship sailing again. **"**

SIR BOBBY ROBSON

takes over HMS Newcastle United

" I'm pretty ecstatic – but I'm pretty numb as well, so I'm a bit of both. **"**

SIR BOBBY ROBSON

after victory at Feyenoord gives Newcastle a chance of qualification for the Champions League second round, 2002

"I can't sit there laughing, can I?
Is that what you want? Ha ha ha – like that?
Oh, penalty, ha ha. Oh, it's saved. Ha ha.
No, it's gone in. Ha ha. What do you expect
me to look like?**"**

SIR BOBBY ROBSON'S

reply to a journalist querying his downcast expression, 2003

❝I've only got two words for how we played out there tonight – not good enough.**❞**

SIR BOBBY ROBSON

❝ We're in a dog fight, and the fight in the dog will get us out of trouble. We are solid behind each other, and through being solid we will get out of trouble and, if that fails, then we will be in trouble, but that's not the situation here. We'll all get in the same rowing boat, and we'll all pick up an oar and we'll row the boat. **❞**

SIR BOBBY ROBSON

in Churchillian mode, 2003

"If you see him stripped, he's like Mike Tyson. But he doesn't bite like Tyson.**"**

SIR BOBBY ROBSON

*on the physique of Titus Bramble – and the fact the only
bite was in his tackling, circa 2003*

"Congratulations, I've heard
a lot about you. But whatever you do,
don't get injured. **"**

New United boss **BOBBY ROBSON**
*meets Kieron Dyer – on the pitch at Wembley before
England v Luxembourg, 1999*

"He's got this terrific little engine, I don't know where he gets his petrol from – I could do with some of that. **"**

SIR BOBBY ROBSON
on Kieron Dyer

" I'm looking for a goalkeeper
with three legs. **"**

SIR BOBBY ROBSON

after Shay Given is nutmegged twice by
Marcus Bent of Ipswich Town

❝ Bellamy came on at Liverpool and did well, but everyone thinks that he's the saviour, that he's Jesus Christ. He's not Jesus Christ. **❞**

SIR BOBBY ROBSON

debunks an unlikely myth...

"There is no hesitation by the club in recording its sincere appreciation for the way in which Sir Bobby has handled team affairs during that five-year spell which has seen a significant turnaround in the club's fortunes.**"**

NEWCASTLE STATEMENT

August 2004

"I was about to enter a period of life
that I can only really describe as a kind
of bereavement. **"**

SIR BOBBY ROBSON

on being sacked in August 2004

"I don't need to be told by anyone that Newcastle are one of the best supported clubs around. Everything is geared to be successful, and I hope I can bring success.**"**

GRAEME SOUNESS

takes over at Newcastle, September 2004

" Sou Long. **"**

THE SUN'S

headline when Souness was sacked, February 2006

"I could sign a bad player every day between now and 31 January. There are plenty out there.**"**

A frustrated **GLENN ROEDER**,
January 2007 transfer window

97

"When they've worked all week, for them the match is a bit like people down south going to the theatre. They want to see something that's worth seeing. Provided it's a really good show, even if it doesn't work out quite the way they wanted, they'll go home thinking, 'That was good'.**"**

Never say never – **KEVIN KEEGAN**
returns to Tyneside, January 2008

❝We're a million miles away from challenging for the league, but if my owner backs me, and I have no proof of that but no doubt he will, we want to try to finish fifth and top of the other mini-league. I get on great with the owner because I never talk to him.**❞**

KENNY DALGLISH,
May 2008 – four games before he left United once again

" I will pick two local papers and speak to them, and the rest can f*ck off. I ain't coming up here to have the p*ss taken out of me. I have a million pages of crap that has been written about me. **"**

JOE KINNEAR'S

expletive-ridden first press conference

"You can see why a lot of big names out there didn't have the arsehole to take this job. You can see why so many people bottled it. **"**

More purple prose from **JOE KINNEAR**

"Shay [Given] pulled out with a knee injury as did Insomnia … Insomnia … er, Charlie.**"**

JOE KINNEAR

tries in vain to pronounce N'Zogbia, who wasn't impressed…

" Everyone at Newcastle United is absolutely delighted that Alan has taken on this challenge. Already there is a buzz around the club and the city. The news has given everyone a massive boost. **"**

DEREK LLAMBIAS

greets Alan Shearer as manager... on April Fools' Day

" He is a very popular choice and it's a little bit of mental doping for the whole Newcastle area because it will give them belief and hope again. **"**

ARSENE WENGER

praises the appointment of Wor Al

❝I wasn't good enough, Mike Ashley wasn't good enough and Chris Hughton, Joe Kinnear and Kevin Keegan before that weren't good enough. But it's what is in the dressing-room that has got us relegated. It has been a problem all season.**❞**

ALAN SHEARER

reacts to Newcastle's Premier League relegation

"He was never a tactical genius, but he did a marvellous job of managing Newcastle United. **"**

FRANK CLARK *on Joe Harvey*

❝All you've got to do is score a goal.
These foreigners are all the same,
they'll collapse like a pack of cards –
they've no gumption. **❞**

JOE HARVEY'S

*inspirational half-time team talk in the Fairs Cup final
second leg, 1969*

"It will haunt me for ever. I feel sick and embarrassed.**"**

JOE HARVEY

speaking about the 1974 FA Cup final humiliation versus Liverpool

"As the manager I have a duty to give them sweat, to give them blood and, to be quite honest, I would die for the club that I worked for.**"**

GORDON LEE

pledges his life to United, literally

"If I've done it wrong, I'm sorry but
I think I did it right and time will show
that I did it right. **"**

An unrepentant **JACK CHARLTON**
interviewed after his resignation as manager

" I'm not going to look beyond
the semi-final – but I would love to lead
Newcastle out at the final. **"**

SIR BOBBY ROBSON

dares to dream – in spite of himself – ahead of the
1998 FA Cup semi-final against Sheffield Wednesday

CHAPTER 4

GAFFERS TAKES: PART 2

More wit and the occasional nugget of wisdom from Magpies bosses, owners and chairmen from down the years...

❝He was a multi-millionaire when I joined Newcastle. Now he's just a millionaire. **❞**

KEVING KEEGAN

explains how he punched a sizeable hole in Sir John Hall's bank balance following the £15m signing of Alan Shearer

"Our fans like people like
Keith Gillesepie – they relate to people
who like to have a drink and get
into trouble.**"**

DOUGLAS HALL,
son of former club owner Sir John Hall, tells it like it is!

115

"You simply do not sack
Bobby Robson. **"**

Former chairman **FREDDY SHEPHERD**
with his classic line – a few days before he did sack Sir Bobby!

" People say you need coaching badges to be a manager, but when I went to Newcastle my only qualification was a thousand rounds of golf in Spain. **"**

KEVIN KEEGAN

and how being a boss was different back in the 1990s…

❝Laurent Robert said I was picking the wrong team. At the time I was, because he was in it. **❞**

SIR BOBBY ROBSON

paints a bleak future for the rebel French winger!

“Manchester United dropped points, Liverpool dropped points, Chelsea dropped points, Everton dropped points, so in a way we haven't lost anything at all really, although we dropped all three.”

Quintessential **SIR BOBBY ROBSON**
as the Toon boss puts an interesting spin on a Newcastle defeat (date unknown)

❝It was the saddest day of my life: he was my very best buy. I could watch him play all day and every day.**❞**

JOE HARVEY *on the day knee ligament trouble forced midfielder Tony Green to quit, December 1973*

❝I took him off because he wasn't hungry enough for his hat-trick.**❞**

Hardman **ARTHUR COX**
explains why he substituted two-goal Chris Waddle, 1983

Alan Shearer has done very well for us, considering his age. We have introduced some movement into his legs because he has got two good legs now. Last season he played with one.

SIR BOBBY ROBSON

reflects on Alan Shearer's ability to play one-legged football, 2004

❝If I had known in advance of the two years of heartache I faced when I moved to Newcastle, I would not have taken the job. **❞**

JOHN HENDRIE,

when asked what made him come to Newcastle in 1988

❝My heart is broken.❞

OSSIE ARDILES

reacts to his sacking as manager, 5 April 1992

"Kevin phoned and said: 'we're going back, pal! We're going to change that club around.'**"**

TERRY MCDERMOTT

recalls the day he got "that" call from Kevin Keegan, 1992

"There's no job in football that I've ever wanted. This is the only job I've ever wanted.**"**

KEVIN KEEGAN

walks out on United over broken promises, March 1992

"It wasn't like it said in the brochure."

KEVIN KEEGAN

Kevin Keegan briefly walks out on the Magpies after becoming
frustrated with Chairman John Hall, March 1992

" We came out of the blocks like a Powderhall sprinter. "

KEVIN KEEGAN

reflects on the run of 11 league wins at the start of 1992–93

NEWCASTLE UNITED

“What a man. What a signing!**”**

KEVIN KEEGAN

reacts to signing Alan Shearer, July 1996

" We'll play you anywhere – Hackney Marshes – we're not frightened. **"**

KENNY DALGLISH

*in a phone call to Stevenage Borough FC after a rumpus over
Broadhall Way's fitness to host an FA Cup tie*

❝We used to have Shaka Hislop on our books, but I've never heard of Shakira. Is she a singer?**❞**

SIR BOBBY ROBSON

*on learning pop queen Shakira was staying in the same
Barcelona hotel as his players, 2002*

"The last exciting piece
of the jigsaw...**"**

KEVIN KEEGAN

upon signing Andy Cole

“If I've got it wrong then there's a
bullet with my name on it. **”**

KEVIN KEEGAN *faces fans the day after selling*
top-scorer Andy Cole

“I've been out of short trousers for a long time now and I'm not going to say this is the worst day of my life.**”**

KENNY DALGLISH

after being sacked, August 1998

"You can't force people to sit down even if they have a seat. They want to sing and, unless you're Val Doonican, you can't do that sitting down. **"**

KEVIN KEEGAN, *1992*

" The circus came to town, but the lions and tigers didn't turn up. **"**

KEVIN KEEGAN

after losing at Old Trafford in December 1995

"I've kept really quiet, but I'll tell you something, he went down in my estimation when he said that. But I'll tell ya – you can tell him now if you're watching it – we're still fighting for this title, and he's got to go to Middlesbrough and get something, and… and I tell you honestly, I will love it if we beat them… love it! **"**

KEVIN KEEGAN

feels the heat coming from Alex Ferguson's direction during the Premiership run-in, 1996

"He's not a player you can tell to do this or do that, you just have to let him get on with it. **"**

KEVIN KEEGAN

after Tino Asprilla's debut, February 1996

"We declare that Kevin Keegan was constructively dismissed by Newcastle United Football Club Limited for which Newcastle United Football Club Limited must pay to Kevin Keegan damages in the sum of £2 million plus interest to be assessed if not agreed. **"**

Judgment in the **KEVIN KEEGAN** *v NUFC court case*

"Ultimately the fans don't support me, they support the shirt.**"**

ALAN PARDEW

after his first game as Newcastle manager, December 2010

❝He is not for sale.
I am going to say it for one last time,
he is not for sale. **❞**

ALAN PARDEW'S *infamous Andy Carroll soundbite*

❝I saw an interview where Alan Pardew said he hoped to get some of that £35 million. I thought: 'Alan, you ain't going to get any of that.'**❞**

KEVIN KEEGAN *twists the knife over the destination of the Andy Carroll transfer fee*

❝When I came, people asked me
if I knew how big the job was.
Now I know what they meant.**❞**

GULLIT *resigns, 28.8.99*

CHAPTER 5

TOON ARMY

A loyal and passionate fanbase who have backed the club in huge numbers through thin and thinner...

NEWCASTLE UNITED

❝We're supposed to be at home!**❞**

NEWCASTLE FANS

singing in Barcelona, 11.12.02, after torrential rain saw their
game postponed for 24 hours

“ This is a club in my heart, it grew that way. It is an amazing city – a tight place where everyone adores the club. It is a one-city club and it is almost unique in the way everyone wears the shirts. You come to the ground and see women, kids, the whole family with their shirts on. **”**

NICKY BUTT

pays tribute to the Toon Army following his retirement

" Radford – now Tudor's gone down
for Newcastle… Radford again, oh what
a goal, what a goal! **"**

JOHN MOTSON

The late Match of the Day *commentator launches his career by
describing Hereford's equaliser in the FA Cup, February 1972*

"Craggs forward, Keegan's flick, Varadi, Keegan again – chance here for Keegan… he's done it! Kevin Keegan scores and St James' Park goes absolutely wild! **"**

Commentator **ROGER TAMES***,*
describing Keegan's debut goal against QPR in 1982

"I queued for five hours at the Gallowgate end to watch Keegan's first match. **"**

ALAN SHEARER,
Newcastle fan

NEWCASTLE UNITED

❝Who's your next Messiah –
Ant or Dec?**❞**

ASTON VILLA
fan banner, May 2009

❝Mike was offered a drink which he thought was non-alcoholic so he took it in good faith.**❞**

Club statement after the former Newcastle owner Mike Ashley is
caught on camera downing a pint at Arsenal's Emirates Stadium

NEWCASTLE UNITED

"The crowd sucked it in.**"**

KEVIN KEEGAN

claims the will of the Newcastle fans has extraordinary powers

" Not a team sheet but a
suicide note. **"**

Journalist **TIM RICH'S**
*comment after Ruud Gullit omits Alan Shearer from his
team to face Sunderland, 1999*

It was f**n' magic! When big Dunc Ferguson scored, I bloody exploded oot me seat, and so did Keegan!**

AC/DC Singer **BRYAN JOHNSON**
recalls a visit to see his beloved black and whites

" In Liverpool you get it from
The Kop, but at St James' Park it
comes from everywhere. It's like stereo
with four speakers! **"**

KEVIN KEEGAN

compares crowd noise at two of his favourite clubs

❝If you put 11 black-and-white dogs on the field at Newcastle you'd get 30,000 coming to watch. **❞**

SIR MATT BUSBY

"I wish we had supporters like Newcastle's. Their supporters are more loyal than ours. One has to be fair – if we'd signed Kevin Keegan, I don't believe we would have had the same reaction through the turnstiles. **"**

Sunderland chairman **TOM COWIE**
and his envy of Tyneside, 1982

" Newcastle fans never cease to amaze me. If there was a trophy for best supporters this lot would win it hands down every year. **"**

ALAN SHEARER

"I'd give all this up tonight if it meant that Newcastle, come twenty to five on Saturday, were still in the Second Division.**"**

JOHN ANDERSON

*after his testimonial match, April 1992, with the club
deep in relegation trouble*

"I picked up an injury and spent quite a lot of time on the bench. One of the supporters knitted me a cushion to sit on, which said, 'Reserved for Brian Kilcline'.**"**

The man also known as **"KILLER"**
on home comforts at St James' Park

" I prefer it in Newcastle, knowing all the people want me here. They look me in the eye and say, 'I want to play with you.' "

DAVID GINOLA

loses something in the translation

"It's like a drug to them, they can't get enough of it. You've got to remember these fans have driven down motorways and watched some really abysmal sides in Newcastle shirts. **"**

KEVIN KEEGAN *tries to explain "Toon Army mania"*

" Newcastle had not won in 29 games and two plus nine is 11. While they were scoring the winning goals, I was running round the outside of the ground 11 times to lift the hoodoo. I arrived late and had no ticket. But the moment I got out of the car and touched the Highbury stadium, Ray Parlour was sent off. **"**

URI GELLER *takes all the credit for ending Newcastle's thirty-game winless run in London, December 2001*

NEWCASTLE UNITED

❝He's got cash to invest. With his contacts abroad, he'll make Newcastle well known. We'll win things under him and we'll also get a global perspective. He's a very nice fellow.❞

SIR JOHN HALL *on* **MIKE ASHLEY**

"We're sh*t – and
we're sick of it.**"**

NEWCASTLE FANS AT WIGAN, *December 2007*

❝I would say Newcastle are the most difficult club to manage in the game, gobbling up managers and spitting them out again with hardly a pause. If they regarded their managers as something more than ships that pass in the night they might achieve the stability and consistency that is the basis of success at any club.**❞**

SIR ALEX FERGUSON

defines Geordie RSI

❝ Cockney Mafia Out! **❞**

Newcastle fans unfurl a banner mid-match
following the departure of Kevin Keegan

" I have the interests of Newcastle United at heart. I have listened to you. You want me out. That is what I am now trying to do but it won't happen overnight and it may not happen at all if a buyer does not come in. You don't need to demonstrate against me again because I have got the message. **"**

Part of **MIKE ASHLEY'S**
"I'm off" 1,644-word statement, September 2008 – but he would stick around for many years after!

" Him and his fat mate (Ashley I presume) should be cacking it if I decide to write a book. There'll be no holding back on those two muppets. **"**

JOEY BARTON

– never one to hold back!

" The board of Newcastle United can today confirm that the club is for sale at the price of £100 million. Interested parties should contact Newcastle United at admin@nufc.co.uk. **"**

A new low posted on the official club website

CHAPTER 6

THE FUTURE IS BLACK AND WHITE...

The committed and wealthy ownership Newcastle United fans were waiting for finally landed in 2021...

" We want to be in the Women's Super League as quickly as we can. **"**

BECKY LANGLEY,

manager of Newcastle United Women, and the shared vision she hopes to make happen, April 2022

Amanda's ambition for both the men's and women's teams is to be winning the Champions League, so there's really no ceiling on where this club can go for the women's and the men's sides.

BECKY LANGLEY,

on the vision owner Amanda Staveley has for the team, April 2022

"We wanted to buy something we could really grow. We looked at a number of big clubs around Europe. And we got the chance to look at Newcastle, while looking at Liverpool. We went there and fell madly in love with the fans, the team and the passion.**"**

Co-owner **AMANDA STAVELEY**, *March 2022*

❝Sometimes it can be difficult to leave the house because everybody recognises me. But they are always so friendly, so loving, not just with me but with everyone in my family, my wife, my dad, my mum. The experience I've had here has been amazing.**❞**

BRUNO GUIMARÃES
– who bleached his hair to be less conspicuous(!), October 2022

"It is one more motivation, but this is only my first full season at Newcastle. There is a long way to go. I love playing here, I love to bond with the fans, and I want to become a legend here.**"**

BRUNO GUIMARÃES – *hoping to fulfil his lofty ambitions at St James' Park, October 2022*

"We need to be mindful internally and focus on what we can control, which is our own thoughts and actions. And not look too far ahead or listen too much to news media and focus on our training and games. This is the toughest league in the world for a reason.**"**

EDDIE HOWE,
tempering expectations – for now, December 2022

" Ever since I started this band, I always used to joke with the boys that one day we might play St James' Park in Newcastle. It's a childhood dream come true. **"**

Singer **SAM FENDER**

announces his first St James' Park gig – and a lifelong dream realised, September 2022

"We did Jools Holland and went straight up to St James'. My saxophone player, Johnny, got on the statue, played Local Hero, and 5,000 Geordies just started singing along. I did about a thousand selfies, got proper mobbed, but everybody was absolutely class and gave us a load of cans, and I'm really hungover. I'm really, really hungover.**"**

SAM FENDER *and Magpies fan reacts to the NUFC takeover, October 2021*

" They didn't disguise that the main objective and challenge was to remain in the Premier League this season but in the seasons coming, the objective is to be in the Champions League and eventually win the Champions League. **"**

BRUNO GUIMARÃES

reveals the talks that convinced him to join the Toon

"I believe in the project. I believe in everything they spoke to me about. I'm really happy to be a part of this project. **"**

BRUNO GUIMARAES

❝We are going to be a club that is going to be a big power in world football.**❞**

BRUNO GUIMARÃES

"It's already a club with a great tradition and beautiful history. I have no doubts about my decision to come to Newcastle.**"**

BRUNO GUIMARÃES

" We can do anything. The season is still young enough for all possibilities to exist for us. I want the fans to believe we can do anything. My attitude won't change, but I've no problem with the supporters dreaming, talking, and speculating about what we can achieve. **"**

Boss **EDDIE HOWE**

encourages the success-starved Toon fans to think big as they move to second in the Premier League, December 2022

" To see the supporters, who have been absolutely incredible for us this year, disappointed and hurt, it hurts bad, and the motivation now is to get back here and win them the trophy they deserve. **"**

EDDIE HOWE

following the 2–0 Carabao Cup final defeat to Manchester United, 2023

" We're not here to be popular,
we're here to compete. **"**

EDDIE HOWE

> **❝**I hope we win something
> before I die. **❞**

Actor **ROBSON GREEN**
reacts to the news of the NUFC takeover, October 2021

❝What is a club in any case? Not the buildings or the directors or the people who are paid to represent it. It's not the television contracts, get-out clauses, marketing departments or executive boxes. It's the noise, the passion…

…the feeling of belonging, the pride in your city. It's a small boy clambering up stadium steps for the very first time, gripping his father's hand, gawping at that hallowed stretch of turf beneath him and, without being able to do a thing about it, falling in love. 🙶

Penultimate words from the late, great **SIR BOBBY ROBSON**

"Howay the lads! **"**

ANT & DEC *end their* Saturday Night Takeaway *show*
with a battle cry for the Toon ahead of the 2023 Carabao Cup final
the following day